Share It! 2

Student Book

Fiona Davis

macmillan education

Scope & Sequence

Welcome to Shareville! pages 4–5	Hi, Hello Character names: Alex, Eva, Nancy, May, Dan, Sam, Sally	I'm … My name's … What's your name? How are you?	*Share It!* Song
	Vocabulary	**Grammar**	**Sharebook**
Unit 1 **On the Farm** pages 10–19	donkey, horse, goat, duck, sheep, cow, chicken caterpillar, butterfly, bee, mosquito, ladybug, ant	What's this / that? It's a … What are these / those? They're …	*Memory Game* Sharebook pages 7, 9 *Find the Insects!* Sharebook page 11
Unit 2 **My Things** pages 20–29	teddy bear, camera, scooter, train, yo-yo, skateboard, board game, video game bag, tablet, paintbrush, scissors, marker, paint, glue, photo	That's his … / That's her … Those are their … Is this your …? Are these your …? Those are our things.	*His or Her?* Sharebook page 13 *My or Your?* Sharebook page 15
Share the World 1	**Story:** *The Ant and The Bird* pages 30–31		
Unit 3 **At the Zoo** pages 34–43	elephant, zebra, giraffe, monkey, hippo, crocodile, tiger beach, bookstore, mall, playground, school, swimming pool, zoo	Is there a monkey? Yes, there is. / No, there isn't. Are there hippos? Yes, there are. / No, there aren't. Where's the playground? It's in front of / behind / between the …	*Is There an Elephant?* Sharebook pages 17, 18 *Hide the Animals!* Sharebook page 19
Unit 4 **Yummy Food** pages 44–53	pineapples, pears, apples, kiwis, watermelons, oranges, coconuts, bananas burger, corn, egg, French fries, pancakes, pie, sandwich, soup	Does Dan like bananas? Yes, he does. / No, he doesn't. What do you want for breakfast? I want eggs and pancakes, please.	*Find Out!* Sharebook page 21 *What Do You Want for Dinner?* Sharebook pages 23, 25
Share the World 2	**Poem:** *Snack Time* pages 54–55		
Unit 5 **I Can Do It!** pages 58–67	fly, write, draw, jump, walk, swim, read, run throw a ball, catch a ball, ride a bike, drive a car, use a computer, play the guitar, jump rope, climb a tree	You can draw and write. I can draw, but I can't fly. Can you / he / she climb a tree? Yes, I can. / No, he can't.	*Can or Can't?* Sharebook pages 27, 29 *Can You Jump Rope?* Sharebook page 31
Unit 6 **My Day** pages 68–77	get up, eat breakfast, go to school, eat lunch, go home, eat dinner, brush my teeth, go to bed eight o'clock, half past nine, a quarter after one, a quarter to two, nine thirty, one fifteen, one forty-five	What do you do in the morning? I eat breakfast. When does he / she go to bed? He / She goes to bed at 8:30.	*I'm Out!* Sharebook page 33 *When?* Sharebook pages 35, 36
Share the World 3	**Blog:** *Village Life, City Life* pages 78–79		
Unit 7 **Playtime!** pages 82–91	playing soccer, playing tennis, watching TV, playing video games, reading books, listening to music, taking photos singing, dancing, writing stories, drawing, playing the piano, playing board games, baking cookies	What do you like doing? I like playing tennis. Do you like playing tennis? What does he / she like doing? He / She likes … Does he / she like …?	*What do You Like Doing?* Sharebook page 37 *Favorite Activities* Sharebook pages 39, 41
Unit 8 **Cool Clothes** pages 92–101	pants, T-shirt, shirt, sweater, sneakers, skirt, shoes, socks dress, jacket, jeans, shorts, baseball cap, hat, boots	Whose sweater is that? It's May's sweater. Whose sneakers are those? They're Dan's sneakers. What are you wearing? What's he / she wearing? I'm / He's / She's wearing …	*Memory Game* Sharebook page 43 *What's Joey Wearing?* Sharebook pages 45, 46
Share the World 4	**Play:** *The Sad Princess* pages 102–103		
Grammar Practice	pages 106–109		

Welcome Unit pages 6–9	**Our Classroom** Monday, Tuesday, Wednesday, Thursday, Friday, Saturday, Sunday Numbers 20–100		What day is it? How many balls are there? There are forty-two balls.
Reading	**CLIL**	**Phonics**	**Progress Tracker**
Story *This Is For You!* **Value** Be kind to animals.	**Science** **Text:** *Bugs Are Great!* wings, open, leaf, closed, bugs, insects **Project:** Make a bug fact card	Short *a*	Review Game: *Round and Round!*
Story *Can I Borrow It?* **Value** Ask first.	**Art** **Text:** *Fun with Colors!* mix, easel, painting, collage **Project:** Make a color wheel	Short *i*	Review Game: *Four in a Row!*
Exam Practice 1 Listening, Reading and Writing pages 32–33			
Story *Follow the Rules!* **Value** Follow the rules.	**Science** **Text:** *Baby Animals* body, tail, hatch, go to sleep, neck, gives **Project:** Draw a picture of animals in nature	Short *o*	Review Game: *Race to Win!*
Story *Try it, Dan!* **Value** Try new things!	**Science** **Text:** *Life Cycle of a Fruit* seed, grows, plant, ground **Project:** Make a life cycle poster for a fruit	Short e	Review Game: *Spin to Win!*
Exam Practice 2 Listening, Reading and Writing pages 56–57			
Story *You Can Do It!* **Value** Encourage others.	**P.E.** **Text:** *Let's Play!* team, net, bounce, basketball, bat, hit, baseball, ice skates, stick, net, hockey **Project:** Draw your favorite sport or activity	Short *u*	Review Game: *Four in a Row!*
Story *I'm on Time!* **Value** Be on time.	**Social Studies** **Text:** *Night and Day* night, asleep, awake, day **Project:** Draw and label a time zone poster	Short vowels	Review Game: *Round and Round!*
Exam Practice 3 Listening, Reading and Writing pages 80–81			
Story *A Good Idea* **Value** Play together!	**Music** **Text:** *Make Some Music!* strings, keys, press, flute, holes, blow **Project:** Design a musical instrument	Short vowels	Review Game: *Spin to Win!*
Story *May's New Clothes* **Value** Take care of your things.	**Art** **Text:** *Something Old, Something New* old, trash, dirty, clean, new, recycled **Project:** Make a collage from recycled materials	Short vowels	Review Game: *Race to Win!*
Exam Practice 4 Listening, Reading and Writing pages 104–105			
Word List pages 110–111			

Welcome to Shareville!

1 1.01 **Read and listen.**

2 1.02 **Listen and sing.**

Share It! Song

Everybody, clap along
Clap your hands to the *Share It* Song!
Let's be fair, and show we care
All together now, let's share!

Come to Shareville, we'll learn today
And make some friends along the way.
We'll share the world, we all belong
Share our voices and all sing this song!

Welcome Unit Our Classroom

1.03 **Listen and read. Then talk about it.**

1 Be respectful.

Speak clearly.

Follow the rules.

2 Be kind.

Help your partner.

Wait your turn.

3 Be responsible.

Check your work.

Put your things away.

2 Read and think. Then write your name.

I promise to be respectful, kind, and responsible.
I promise to follow our classroom rules.

Name: ______________________

Workbook page 4

3 1.04 **Listen, point, and say. Then quiz a friend.**

1. Monday
2. Tuesday
3. Wednesday
4. Thursday
5. Friday
6. Saturday
7. Sunday

4 1.05 **Listen and point. Then sing.**

What Day Is It?

What day is it? What day is it?
What day is it today?

M is for Monday, mouse, and me.
T is for Tuesday, teacher, and tree.
I like Wednesdays. How about you?
Wednesday starts with a W.

What day is it? What day is it?
What day is it today?

T-H is for Thursday, thanks, and three.
F is for Friday, fingers, and feet.
I like weekends. How about you?
S is for Saturday, and Sunday, too!

5 1.06 **Listen, read, and say.**

Workbook page 5

I can name the days of the week. ☐

Numbers 20–100

6 1.07 **Listen, point, and say. Then quiz a friend.**

7 1.08 **Listen and point. Then chant.**

8 1.09 **Listen, read, and say.**

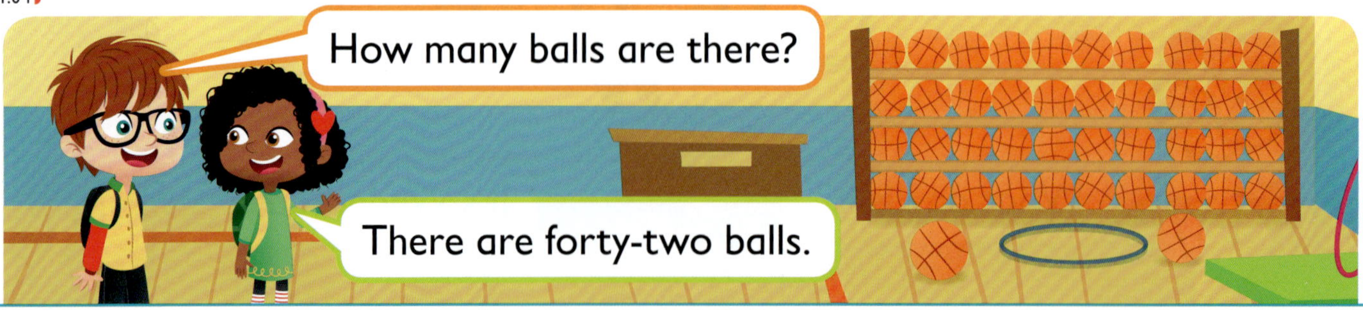

I can count to 100. ☐

Workbook page 6

9 Find, point, and name. Then check (✓).

1 one Share Pal ☐
2 two jobs ☐
3 three drinks ☐
4 four animals ☐
5 five children ☐
6 six foods ☐
7 seven toys ☐
8 eight school things ☐
9 nine body parts ☐
10 ten colors ☐

10 Look and match. Then ask and answer.

1 What color are the flowers?
2 How old is Dan?
3 Where's the bird?
4 Does Sam have a book?
5 Does May have long hair?

a He's eight.
b No, he doesn't.
c It's on the chair.
d Yes, she does.
e They're yellow.

I can use the language in Student Book 1. ☐

1 On the Farm

Lesson 1 Vocabulary

1 **Talk about the picture.**

Who do you see?

I see May.

2 1.10 **Listen, point, and say. Then quiz a friend.**

3 1.11 **Listen and point. Then chant.**

A sheep, a goat,
A black and white cow,
A duck and a chicken
Are on the farm now.

A sheep, a goat,
A black and white cow,
A horse and a donkey
Are on the farm now.

 I can name farm animals. ☐ Workbook page 8

Lesson 2 Grammar

1 1.12 **Listen to May and Dan. Read and say.**

Grammar

What's **this**? It'**s** a goat.

What's **that**? It'**s** a duck.

What'**s** = What **is**

Grammar Practice page 106

2 1.13 **Listen to May. Then say the animal.**

3 Sharebook A: page 7 B: page 9

Memory Game

I can talk about farm animals. ☐

Lesson 3 Story This Is for You!

1 **Look and answer. What animals can you see?**

2 **Read the story. Then act.**

1.14

Value
Be kind to animals.

3 Look, read, and write *Yes* or *No*.

1 Dan is kind to the black sheep. ______

2 Nancy is kind to the baby duck. ______

3 Dan is kind to the cat. ______

Workbook page 10

I can read the story. ☐

Lesson 4 Vocabulary

1 (1.15) **Listen, point, and say. Then quiz a friend.**

1 caterpillar

2 butterfly

3 bee

4 mosquito

5 ladybug

6 ant

2 (1.16) **Listen and circle. Then sing.**

What's This? What's That?

What's this in my hand?
Is it a caterpillar or an ant?
Is it a spider? Or a snake?
What's this in my hand?
It's a  /  !

What's that in the tree?
Is it a butterfly or a bee?
Is it a ladybug? Or a mosquito?
What's that in the tree?
It's a  /  !

3 **Draw and guess!**

What's this?

Is it a butterfly?

Yes, it is!

I can name insects. ☐

Workbook page 11

1 Listen, read, and say.
1.17

Grammar

What are **these**?

They're caterpillar**s**.

What are **those**?

They're mosquito**s**.

Grammar Practice page 106

2 Listen, look, and answer.
1.18

1 2 3 4

3 Sharebook
A: page 11
B: page 11

Find the Insects!

Workbook page 12

I can ask and answer about insects. ☐

Lesson 6 Science

CLIL

1 Look. What bugs can you see?

2 Read the text. How many legs do the bugs have? 1.19

Bugs Are Great!

1 Spiders have eight legs. They have eight eyes, too. Look!

2 This butterfly has blue and orange **wings**. The wings are **open**. It has six legs.

3 What's this? Is it a **leaf**? No, it's the butterfly. Now the wings are **closed**.

4 A bee is yellow, brown, and black. It has six legs, five eyes, and four wings.

5 You can find **bugs** and **insects** in your yard or in the park. Look on trees, in flowers, and under leaves. How many can you find?

I can read about bugs and insects. ☐

Workbook page 13

1 (1.20) **Read the text again.**

2 **Read and write *True* or *False*.**

1 A spider has six legs. ______

2 A bee has six legs. ______

3 A butterfly has wings. ______

4 A bee has two eyes. ______

3 **Project** **Make a bug fact card.**

4 **Share it!** **Talk about your bug fact card.**

It's a ladybug. It has wings. It's red and black.

Share at Home
Tell your family about six different bugs.

Workbook page 14

I can share my bug fact card. ☐

Lesson 8 Phonics Short *a*

1 1.21 **Listen, point, and chant.**

1

s**a**d

2

h**a**t

3

m**a**d

4

m**a**n

5

c**a**t

6

b**a**t

2 1.22 **Listen and repeat. Then read and say.**

1	at	sat	hat	bat
2	an	man	can	cat

REVIEW

3	a	e	i	o	u

3 1.23 **Listen, read, and say.**

I am sad.

Dad has a black hat.

I can read and say words with the short *a* sound. ☐

Workbook page 15

Progress Tracker

1 Play *Round and Round!* Use the language from Unit 1.

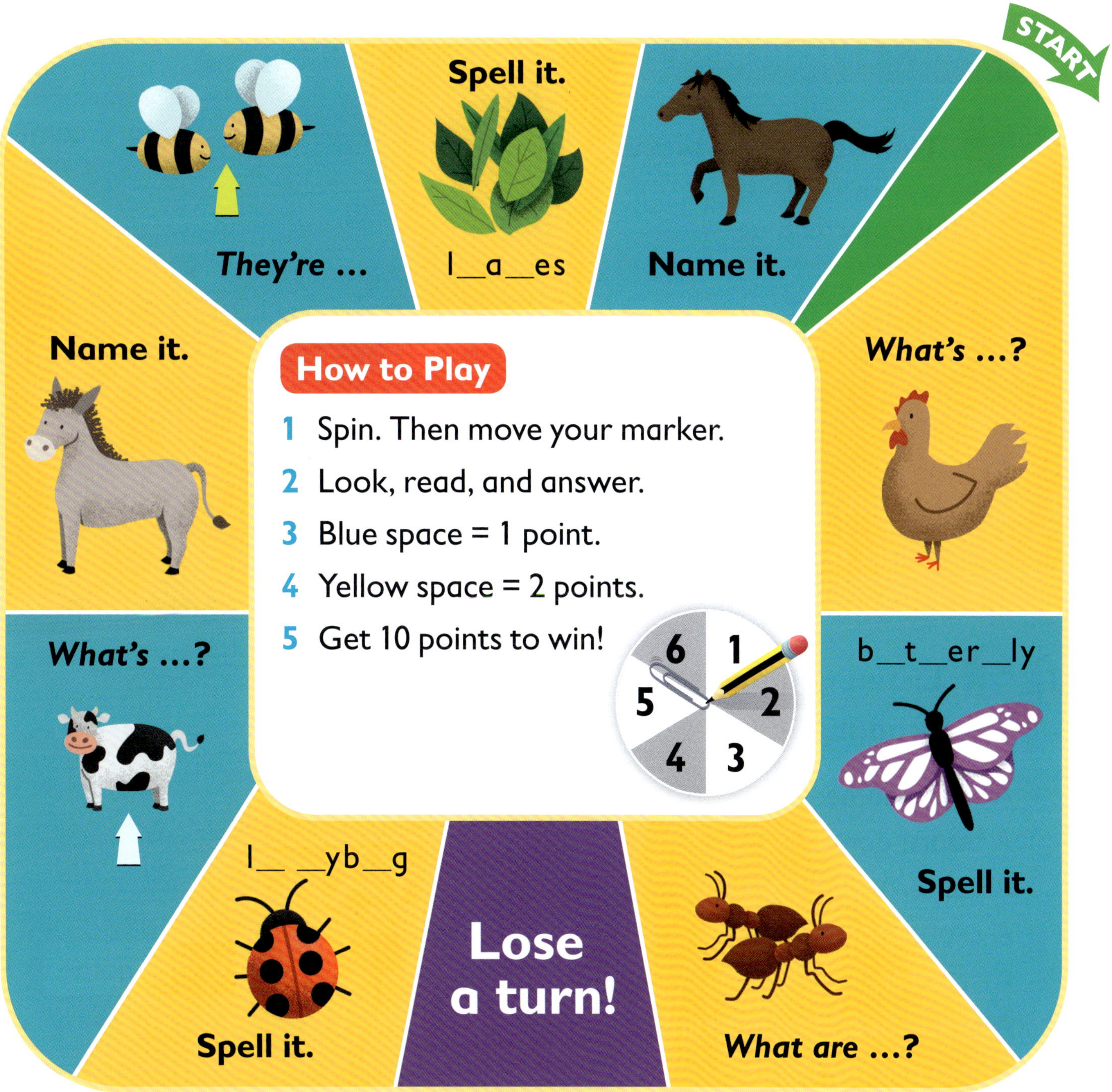

How to Play

1 Spin. Then move your marker.
2 Look, read, and answer.
3 Blue space = 1 point.
4 Yellow space = 2 points.
5 Get 10 points to win!

2 Now complete your Progress Tracker in the Workbook.

Workbook page 16

I can use the language in Unit 1. ☐

2 My Things

Lesson 1 Vocabulary

1 **Talk about the picture.**

What color is that?

It's green.

2 1.24 **Listen, point, and say. Then quiz a friend.**

3 1.25 **Listen and point. Then chant.**

A video game,
A board game,
A camera, and a yo-yo!
A skateboard,
A scooter,
A teddy bear, and a train!
These are my things.
Let's say it again!

 I can name toys and things. ☐ Workbook page 17

Lesson 2 Grammar

1 1.26 **Listen to Nancy and May. Read and say.**

Grammar

That's **his** camera.

Those are **her** teddy bears.

Those are **their** yo-yos.

Grammar Practice page 106

2 **Look at the picture. Play *Sentence Tennis*.**

That's his train.

Those are her board games.

3 **Sharebook** A: pages 13–14 B: pages 13–14

His or Her?

That's his camera.

No, that's her camera.

Workbook page 18

I can talk about people's toys and things. ☐

Lesson 3 Story Can I Borrow It?

1 Look and answer. Who has a skateboard?

2 (1.27) **Read the story. Then act.**

Value
Ask first.

3 Look, read, and write.

I like your yo-yo! ________ I ____________ it?

Sure!

Lesson 4 Vocabulary

1 1.28 **Listen, point, and say. Then quiz a friend.**

1 bag

2 tablet

3 paintbrush

4 scissors

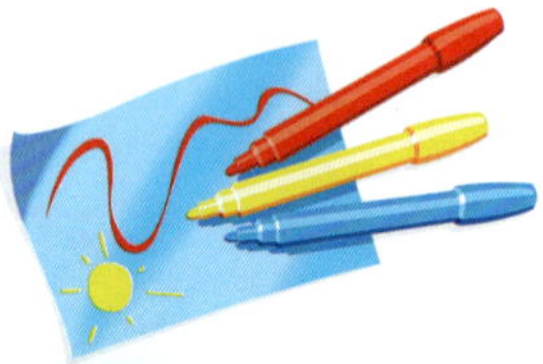

5 marker

6 paint

7 glue

8 photo

2 1.29 **Listen and write. Then sing.**

What's in My Bag?

This is my bag. These are my things.
What's in my bag? Look and sing!
I have a ____________ and paint,
And ____________ and glue!
These are my school things.
How about you?

This is my bag. These are my things!
What's in my bag? Look and sing!
I have a ____________ and a paintbrush,
And a ____________ of you!
These are my school things.
How about you?

3 **Draw and guess!**

Is it a photo?

No, it isn't. It's a tablet!

 I can name school things. ☐

Workbook page 20

1 Listen, read, and say.
1.30

Grammar

Is this **your** bag?

Are these **your** scissors?

Those are **our** things.

Grammar Practice page 106

2 Listen and check (✔) Lucy's things.
1.31

1 

2 

3 

4 

3 Sharebook A: page 15 B: page 15 *My or Your?*

I can ask and answer about school things. ☐

Lesson 6 Art

CLIL

1 Look. How many colors can you see?

2 Read the text. What colors make green?

1.32

Fun with Colors!

1 This is a color wheel. Can you name the colors on it?

2 You can **mix** colors.
Mix blue and yellow to make green.
Mix red and yellow to make orange.
Mix red and blue to make purple.

3 This artist is at her **easel**. This is her **painting**. She uses paint and a paintbrush to make it.

4 This picture is a **collage**. You can make a collage with paint, paper, scissors, and glue.

There are a lot of colors in the collage. What colors can you see? Find the colors on the color wheel!

I can read about colors and pictures. ☐

Workbook page 22

1 Read the text again. 1.33

2 **Read and write *True* or *False*.**

1 Yellow and green make orange. ______

2 You can make a collage with paint, paper, scissors, and glue. ______

3 Yellow and blue make green. ______

3 **Project** **Make a color wheel.**

4 **Share it!** **Talk about your color wheel.**

This is my color wheel. Red and blue make purple.

Share at Home

Tell your family about three colors on the color wheel. How can you make them?

I can share my color wheel. ☐

Lesson 8 Phonics Short *i*

1 Listen, point, and chant.

1.34

1

six

2

sit

3

big

4

kick

5

rip

6

wigs

2 Listen and repeat. Then read and say.

1.35

1	is	it	sit	hit
2	in	win	wig	wigs
REVIEW 3	can	sad	dad	man

3 Listen, read, and say.

1.36

He hit it.

We win!

I can read and say words with the short *i* sound. ☐

Workbook page 24

1 Play *Four in a Row!* Use the language from Unit 2.

Is this her …?	**Name it.**	*That's his …*	**Spell it.** p__in__bru__h
Spell it. m__ __k__r	*Those are my …*	**Name it.**	*Is this her …?* JESSICA
Name it.	*Is this his …?*	**Spell it.** __ai__ti__g	*Those are his …*
That's her …	**Spell it.** p__ot__	*Are those your …?*	**Name it.**

How to Play

1 Collect eight markers.
2 Choose a space. Look, read, and answer.
3 Put a marker on the space.
4 Get four markers in a row to win.

2 **Now complete your Progress Tracker in the Workbook.**

Workbook page 25

I can use the language in Unit 2. ☐

Share the World 1

The Ant and The Bird

1 Look at the pictures. Which animals and insects can you see?

2 1.37 **Read the story. Who are new friends?**

3 Read the story again. Then answer. Use *the ant*, *the bird*, or *the men*.

1 Who is thirsty? ______________________

2 Who has a net? ______________________

3 Who says "Thank you"? ______________________

4 Share Your World **What's your favorite part of the story? Draw it in your Workbook.**

Workbook pages 26–27

YLE Starters

Exam Practice 1

Listening

1 (1.38) **Listen and draw lines. There is one example.**

Jill Alice Lucy Ben

Kim Mark Hugo

Reading and Writing

2 Look and read. Write *yes* or *no*. There are two examples.

Examples

There is a brown horse. ......yes......

The farmer has gray hair. ......no......

Questions

1 The girl has a scooter. ....

2 There is a boy in the tree. ....

3 There are butterflies on the flowers. ....

4 Three ducks are next to the water. ....

5 There are two cows. ....

3 At the Zoo

Lesson 1 Vocabulary

1 **Talk about the picture.**

How many people are there?

Eight.

2 1.39 **Listen, point, and say. Then quiz a friend.**

3 1.40 **Listen and point. Then chant.**

Giraffes and an elephant!
Tigers and hippos, too!
I love the animals
At the zoo!

Zebras and a crocodile!
Look! A monkey, too!
I love the animals
At the zoo!

 I can name zoo animals. ☐

Workbook page 28

Lesson 2 Grammar

1 1.41 **Listen to Alex and Nancy. Read and say.**

Grammar

Is there a monkey?

Yes, **there is**. / No, **there isn't**.

Are there hippo**s**?

Yes, **there are**. / No, **there aren't**.

Grammar Practice page 107

2 1.42 **Look at the picture. Listen and answer.**

Are there zebras?

Yes, there are.

3 **Sharebook** A: page 17 B: page 18

Is There an Elephant?

Is there an elephant in Number 10?

No, there isn't.

I can talk about zoo animals. ☐

Lesson 3 Story Follow the Rules!

1 Look and answer. What animals can you see?

2 (1.43) **Read the story. Then act.**

Value
Follow the rules.

3 Look, read, and write.

1 What animals like plants? ______________________

2 What is bad for elephants? ______________________

3 Who doesn't follow the rules? ______________________

Workbook page 30

I can read the story. ☐

Lesson 4 Vocabulary

1 1.44 **Listen, point, and say. Then quiz a friend.**

1 beach

2 bookstore

3 mall

4 playground

5 school

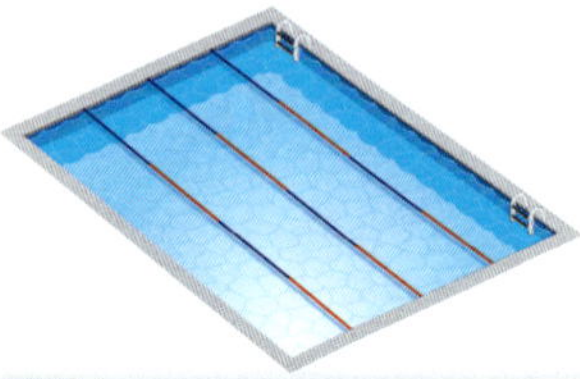

6 swimming pool

7 zoo

2 1.45 **Listen and number. Then sing.**

Animals in Town!

Are there tigers at the [1]?
Are there tigers at the [2]?
Are there tigers at the [3]?
No, no, no!
There are tigers at the [4]! Yahoo!

Is there a hippo at the [5]?
Is there a hippo at the [6]?
Is there a hippo at the [7]?
No, no, no!
There's a hippo at the [8]! Yahoo!

3 **Choose a place. Mime and guess!**

Are you at the swimming pool?

Yes, I am!

 I can name places. ☐

Workbook page 31

1 Listen, read, and say.

1.46

in front of behind between

Grammar

Where's the playground?
It's **in front of** the zoo.
Where's the bookstore?
It's **behind** the zoo.
It's **between** the zoo and the mall.

Grammar Practice page 107

2 Listen and number.

1.47

a

b

c

3 Sharebook

A: page 19
B: page 19

Hide the Animals!

Workbook page 32

I can ask and answer about places. ☐

Lesson 6 Science CLIL

1 **Look. How many babies are there?**

2 (1.48) **Read the text. Which animal eats leaves?**

Baby Animals

1 This crocodile is very long. Her **body** is about three meters from her head to her **tail**! She is a good mother. Her babies **hatch** from eggs.

WOW!
Giraffes don't sit down when they *go to sleep*. They stand up!

2 This baby giraffe is 1.6 meters tall! Giraffes have very long legs and a long **neck**. The mother giraffe eats leaves from the trees. She **gives** milk to her baby.

3 Look at the baby monkey. It has two arms, two legs, and a very long tail! Monkeys climb trees with their arms, legs, and tails.

 I can read about baby animals. ☐

Workbook page 33

1 Read the text again. 1.49

2 Read and circle.

1 A **crocodile** / **monkey** has eggs.

2 A mother **giraffe** / **crocodile** gives milk to her baby.

3 A monkey has a long **body** / **tail**.

3 Project **Draw a picture of animals in nature.**

4 Share it! **Talk about your picture.**

These are giraffes. They eat leaves.

Share at Home
Talk about five different animals.

Workbook page 34

I can share my animal picture. ☐

Lesson 8 Phonics | Short *o*

1 Listen, point, and chant.
1.50

1 
dog

2 
socks

3 
boxes

4 
hop

5 
mom

6 
hot

2 Listen and repeat. Then read and say.
1.51

1	hot	hop	top	mop
2	box	boxes	fox	foxes

REVIEW

3	big	kick	cat	mad

3 Listen, read, and say.
1.52

The fox is on top.

Mom has a mop.

 I can read and say words with the short *o* sound. ☐ Workbook page 35

1 Play *Race to Win!* Use the language from Unit 3.

How to Play

1 Flip a coin. Move one or two spaces.

2 Look, read, and answer.

3 Don't know? Lose a turn.

4 Finish first to win!

move one space

move two spaces

2 **Now complete your Progress Tracker in the Workbook.**

Workbook page 36

I can use the language in Unit 3. ☐

4 Yummy Food!

Lesson 1 Vocabulary

1 **Talk about the picture.**

Where's Alex?

He's next to Nancy.

2 (2.01) **Listen, point, and say. Then quiz a friend.**

3 (2.02) **Listen and point. Then chant.**

Watermelons, watermelons,
Coconuts and pears.
Apples and oranges,
We can share!

Pineapples, pineapples,
Coconuts and pears.
Bananas and kiwis,
We can share!

Workbook page 37

Lesson 2 Grammar

1 2.03 **Listen to Nancy and Alex. Read and say.**

Grammar

Does Dan **like** bananas?

Yes, he **does**. / No, he **doesn't**.

does**n't** = **does not**

Grammar Practice page 107

2 2.04 **Look at the picture. Listen and answer.**

Does Nancy like apples?

Yes, she does.

3 **Sharebook** A: page 21 B: page 21

Find Out!

Does she like pears?

Yes, she does!

I can ask and answer about likes. ☐

Lesson 3 Story Try It, Dan!

1 **Look and answer. How many cakes are there?**

2 (2.05) **Read the story. Then act.**

Value
Try new things!

3 Circle. Who tries ice-cream cake?

1 

2 

3 

4 

I can read the story. ☐

Lesson 4 Vocabulary

1 2.06 Listen, point, and say. Then quiz a friend.

1 burger

2 corn

3 egg

4 French fries

5 pancakes

6 pie

7 sandwich

8 soup

2 2.07 Listen and write. Then sing.

A Yummy Treat

1 Does he want ______________
and ______________?
What does he want to eat?

2 Does he want a ______________
and ______________?
What does he want to eat?

3 Does he want a ______________
and ______________?
What does he want to eat?

4 Does he want ______________
and ______________?
What does he want to eat?

3 Talk about food. Then guess.

It has bread and meat.

It's a burger!

1 Listen, read, and say.
2.08

2 Listen and check (✔).
2.09

a  ☐

b  ☐

c  ☐

d  ☐

e  ☐

f  ☐

Grammar

What **do** you **want** for breakfast?
lunch?
dinner?

I **want** eggs and pancakes, please.

Grammar Practice page 107

3 Sharebook
A: page 23
B: page 25

What Do You Want for Dinner?

What do you want for dinner?

I want a burger and pie, please.

I can ask and answer about food. ☐

Lesson 6 Science

CLIL

1 **Look. What fruit do you see?**

2 (2.10) **Read the text. What grows into a plant?**

Life Cycle of a Fruit

1 This is a watermelon farm. Many people like watermelons. They're a very healthy fruit. You can read about watermelons here. They're yummy!

2 This is the life cycle of a watermelon.

1 A watermelon **seed** is black. It **grows** into a **plant**.

2 The plant is green. It grows big.

3 The plant grows flowers.

4 Then the plant has fruit.

5 The fruit has seeds.

6 Now the seeds are on the **ground**. They grow into more watermelons.

3 Watermelons are green and red. They are also very big! Watermelons have a lot of juice. You can drink the juice.

4 I love watermelons!

What's your favorite fruit?

 I can read about the life cycle of a fruit. ☐

Workbook page 42

1 (2.11) **Read the text again.**

2 Look and match.

1 

2 

3 

a a watermelon flower

b watermelon seeds

c a watermelon plant

3 Project Make a life cycle poster for a fruit.

4 Share it! Talk about your life cycle poster.

These are the seeds.

Share at Home

Talk about the life cycle of your favorite fruit.

Workbook page 43

I can share my life cycle poster. ☐

Lesson 8 Phonics Short *e*

1 (2.12) Listen, point, and chant.

1 

ten

2 
egg

3 
bed

4 
bell

5 
yell

6 
wet

2 (2.13) Listen and repeat. Then read and say.

1	ten	hen	pen	red
2	bell	yell	fell	mess
REVIEW 3	mom	hot	kick	sad

3 (2.14) Listen, read, and say.

The bed is a mess.

I see ten hens.

I can read and say words with the short *e* sound. ☐

Workbook page 44

Progress Tracker

1 **Play *Spin to Win!* Use the language from Unit 4.**

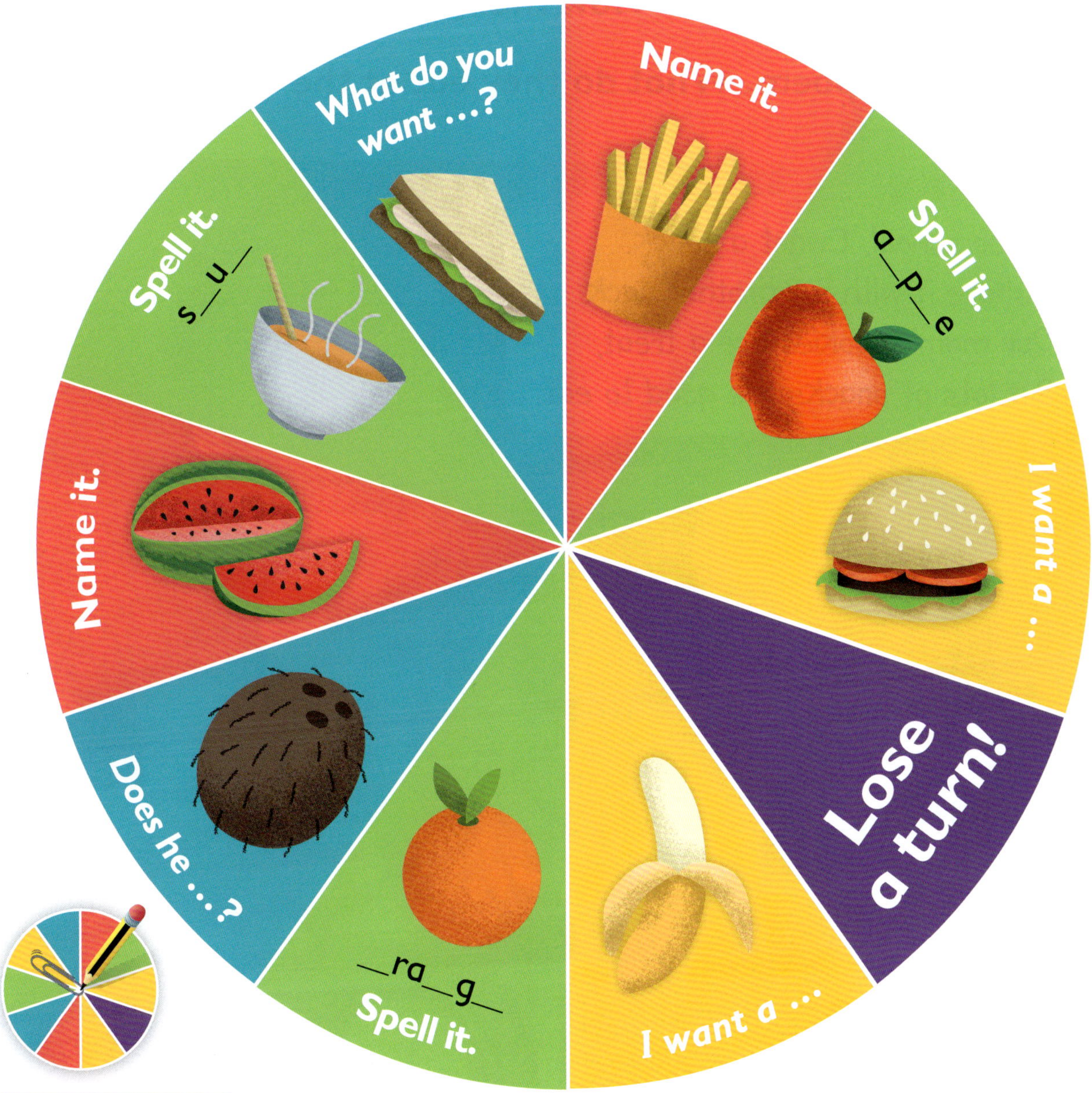

How to Play

1 Spin with a pencil and paper clip.

2 Look, read, and answer.

3 Don't know? Lose a turn.

4 Get six correct answers to win!

2 **Now complete your Progress Tracker in the Workbook.**

I can use the language in Unit 4. ☐

Share the World 2

Snack Time

1 **Look at the pictures. How many snacks are there?**

2 **Read the poem. What do they eat at the store?**
2.15

1 After school, I want a snack.
I share it with my brother Jack.
Our mom's cookies are a treat,
But lots of snacks are good to eat.

2 By the sea, on the sand,
Yellow corn is in my hand.

3 In the park, with the bees,
Two or three more cookies, please!

4 At the store, a bag of grapes!
At my house, chocolate cake!

5 At the zoo, in the sun,
I like ice cream – it's fun!

6 After school, I want a snack.
I share it with my brother Jack.
Milk and cookies are a treat.
What snacks do you like to eat?

3 Read and circle the answer.

1 What is the poem about? snacks / ice cream

2 What is the boy's name? Jack / John

3 What color is the corn? white / yellow

4 Which snack is fun in the sun? grapes / ice cream

4 Share Your World What's your favorite snack? Where do you eat it? Draw it in your Workbook.

Workbook pages 46–47

YLE Starters

Exam Practice 2

Listening

1 (2.16) **Read the question. Listen and write a name or number. There are two examples.**

Examples

What is the new boy's name?	Matt
How many brothers does the new boy have?	2

Questions

1 What is Matt's last name?	....
2 Where does Matt live?	on .... Street
3 What number is Matt's house?	....
4 What does Matt want for lunch?	....
5 How old is Matt?	....

Reading and Writing

2 Look at the pictures. Look at the letters. Write the words.

Example

s h e e p

Questions

1 

....

2 

....

3 

....

4 

....

5 

....

5 I Can Do It!

Lesson 1 Vocabulary

1 **Talk about the picture.**

Where's Eva?

She's on the swing.

2 (2.17) **Listen, point, and say. Then quiz a friend.**

3 (2.18) **Listen and point. Then chant.**

Let's walk and jump,
And swing and slide!
Let's run today! Hey! Hey!

Let's read and write,
And draw and swim!
Let's fly today! Hooray!

 I can name actions. ☐

Workbook page 48

Lesson 2 Grammar

1 2.19 **Listen to Nancy and Dan. Read and say.**

Grammar

You **can** draw **and** write.

I **can** draw, **but** I **can't** fly.

can**'t** = **cannot**

Grammar Practice page 108

2 2.20 **Look at the picture. Listen and say *True* or *False*.**

3 **Sharebook** A: page 27 B: page 29

***Can* or *Can't*?**

Lesson 3 Story You Can Do It!

1 **Look and answer. Who helps Dan?**

2 (2.21) **Read the story. Then act.**

Value
Encourage others.

3 Look, read, and write.

1 Good __________, Dan!

2 You __________ do it!

3 Go, Dan, __________!

I can read the story. ☐

Lesson 4 Vocabulary

1 (2.22) **Listen, point, and say. Then quiz a friend.**

1 throw a ball

2 catch a ball

3 ride a bike

4 drive a car

5 use a computer

6 play the guitar

7 jump rope

8 climb a tree

2 (2.23) **Listen and circle. Then mime and sing.**

Yes, I Can!

I can  /  .

Yes, I can! Yes, I can!

I can  /  and climb a tree.

I can  /  ,

A very big computer!

But I can't jump rope.

No, I can't!

I can  /  .

Yes, I can! Yes, I can!

I can  /  and climb a tree.

I can drive a toy car,

A very small car!

But I can't jump rope.

No, I can't!

3 **Mime an activity. Guess!**

You can play the guitar!

Yes, I can.

I can name activities. ☐

Workbook page 51

1 Listen, read, and say.

2.24

2 Listen, look, and answer.

2.25

1

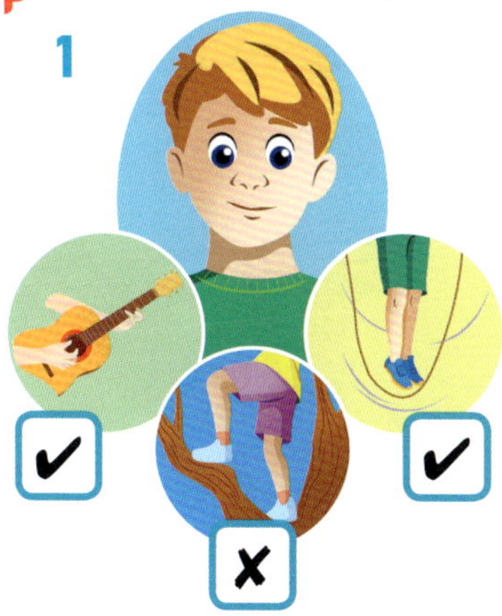

2

Grammar

Can you / he / she **climb** a tree?

Yes, I / he / she **can**.

No, I / he / she **can't**.

Grammar Practice page 108

3 Sharebook

A: page 31
B: page 31

Can You Jump Rope?

 I can ask and answer about a friend's abilities. ☐

Lesson 6 P.E. CLIL

1 **Look. Do all the sports use a ball?**

2 **Read the text. Match the sports to the photos.** 2.26

Let's Play!

1 This sport has five boys or girls on a **team**. They use a big ball and a very tall **net**.

Can you throw and **bounce** a ball? **Basketball** is for you! ☐

2 This sport has nine girls or boys on a team. They use a small white ball and a **bat**.

Can you **hit** and catch a ball? **Baseball** is for you! ☐

3 This sport has six boys or girls on a team. They use **ice skates**, a hockey **stick**, and a **net**.

Can you skate? **Hockey** is for you! ☐

a

b

c

 I can read about sports. ☐

Workbook page 53

1 Read the text again. 2.27

2 Answer the questions. Write.

1 What sport has nine boys or girls on a team? ______

2 In which sport do you bounce a ball? ______

3 Which sports use a net? ______ ______

3 **Project** Draw and label your favorite sport or activity.

4 **Share it!** Talk about your favorite sport.

My favorite sport is baseball. This is the bat.

Share at Home
Talk about six sports or activities you do together.

Workbook page 54

I can share my favorite sport or activity. ☐

Lesson 8 Phonics Short *u*

1 Listen, point, and chant.
2.28

1

bus

2

bug

3

run

4

duck

5

sun

6

cup

2 Listen and repeat. Then read and say.
2.29

1	sun	fun	run	rug
2	up	cup	cub	tub

REVIEW

3	bed	dog	six	man

3 Listen, read, and say.
2.30

The cub's mom is mad.

The sun is hot.

I can read and say words with the short *u* sound. ☐

Workbook page 55

1 Play *Four in a Row!* Use the language from Unit 5.

How to Play

1 Collect eight markers.
2 Choose a space. Look, read, and answer.
3 Put a marker on the space.
4 Get four markers in a row to win.

2 **Now complete your Progress Tracker in the Workbook.**

I can use the language in Unit 5. ☐

6 My Day

Lesson 1 Vocabulary

1 **Talk about the picture.**

Can Sally write?

Yes, she can.

2 2.31 **Listen, point, and say. Then quiz a friend.**

3 2.32 **Listen and point. Then chant.**

Every day I get up,
Eat breakfast, go to school!
Every day I eat lunch,
I go home and play!
Every day I eat dinner,
Brush my teeth, go to bed!
This is my day! Every day!

 I can name my daily routine. ☐

Workbook page 57

Lesson 2 Grammar

1 2.33 **Listen to Miss Summers and Alex. Read and say.**

Grammar

What do you do in the morning?
afternoon?
evening?

I **eat** breakfast. I **go** to school.

Grammar Practice page 108

2 2.34 **Look at the picture. Listen and say *True* or *False*.**

3 Sharebook A: page 33 B: page 33

I'm Out!

I can ask and answer about daily routines. ☐

Lesson 3 Story I'm on Time!

1 **Look and answer. What does Alex like for breakfast?**

2 (2.35) **Read the story. Then act.**

Value
Be on time.

3 Look, read, and write.

It's __________ to get up!

Good. I'm on __________!

I can read the story. ☐

Lesson 4 Vocabulary

1 2.36 **Listen, point, and say. Then quiz a friend.**

1 eight o'clock

2 half past nine

3 a quarter after one

4 a quarter to two

5 nine thirty

6 one fifteen

7 one forty-five

2 2.37 **Listen and write the time. Then sing.**

Tick, Tock!

1 Tick, tock! Tick, tock!
What time is it? It's ________.
What do you do at ________,
At ________ in the morning?

2 Tick, tock! Tick, tock!
What time is it? It's ________.
What do you do at ________,
At ________ in the afternoon?

3 Tick, tock! Tick, tock!
What time is it? It's ________.
What do you do at ________,
At ________ in the evening?

3 **Draw and say.**

What time is it?

It's half past two.

I can say the time. ☐

Workbook page 60

1 Listen, read, and say.

2.38

2 Listen and number.

2.39

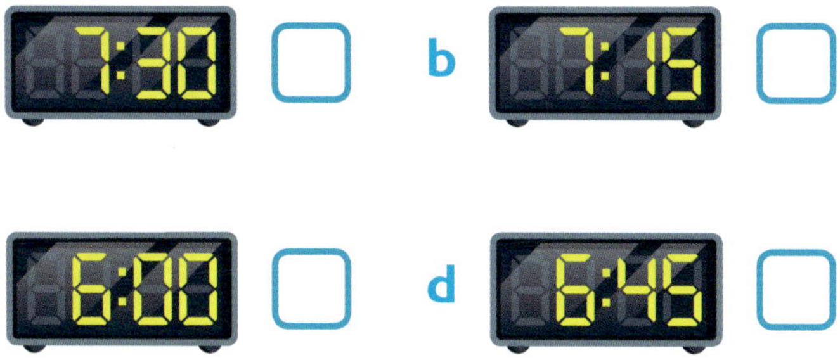

Grammar

When **do** you **go** to bed?
I **go** to bed at 8:30.
When **does** he / she go to bed?
He / She **goes** to bed at 8:30.

Grammar Practice page 108

3 Sharebook

A: page 35
B: page 36

When?

I can ask and answer about the time. ☐

Lesson 6 Social Studies

CLIL

1 Look. Where do the children live?

2 Read the text. Who eats breakfast at 7:30?

2.40

Night and Day

1 Hiro is from Japan. He lives in Tokyo. Megan is from Canada. She lives in Toronto.

Tokyo

2 Right now it's **night** in Japan, but in Canada it's morning. Hiro is **asleep** and Megan is **awake**. Megan eats breakfast at 7:00 every **day**. She goes to school at 8:30. She likes to play sports at school. She goes home at 3:30.

Toronto

Tokyo

3 Now it's morning in Japan, but it's night in Canada. Hiro is awake and Megan is asleep. Hiro eats breakfast at 7:30 every day. He goes to school at 8:30. He likes sports, too. He goes home at 3:00.

Toronto

4 Hiro and Megan live in different time zones, but their days are almost the same!

I can read about children in two time zones. ☐

Workbook page 62

1 2.41 **Read the text again.**

2 Read and circle.

1 It's night in Japan. It's **day** / **night** in Canada.

2 It's morning in Japan. It's **morning** / **night** in Canada.

3 Megan is awake in Canada. Hiro is **awake** / **asleep** in Japan.

3 Project Draw and label a time zone poster.

4 Share it! Talk about your time zone poster.

Right here it's eight o'clock in the evening.

Share at Home
Talk about time zones with your family.

Workbook page 63

I can share my time zone poster. ☐

Lesson 8 Phonics Short vowels

1 Listen, point, and chant.

2.42

1

cut

2

lick

3

leg

4

rock

5

mat

6

bag

2 Listen and repeat. Then read and say.

2.43

1	cut	cuts	yell	yells
2	runs	sits	hops	hits

REVIEW

3	up	red	black	mom

3 Listen, read, and say.

2.44

The frog hops.

She gets up at six.

I can read and say words with short vowel sounds. ☐

Workbook page 64

1 **Play *Round and Round!* Use the language from Unit 6.**

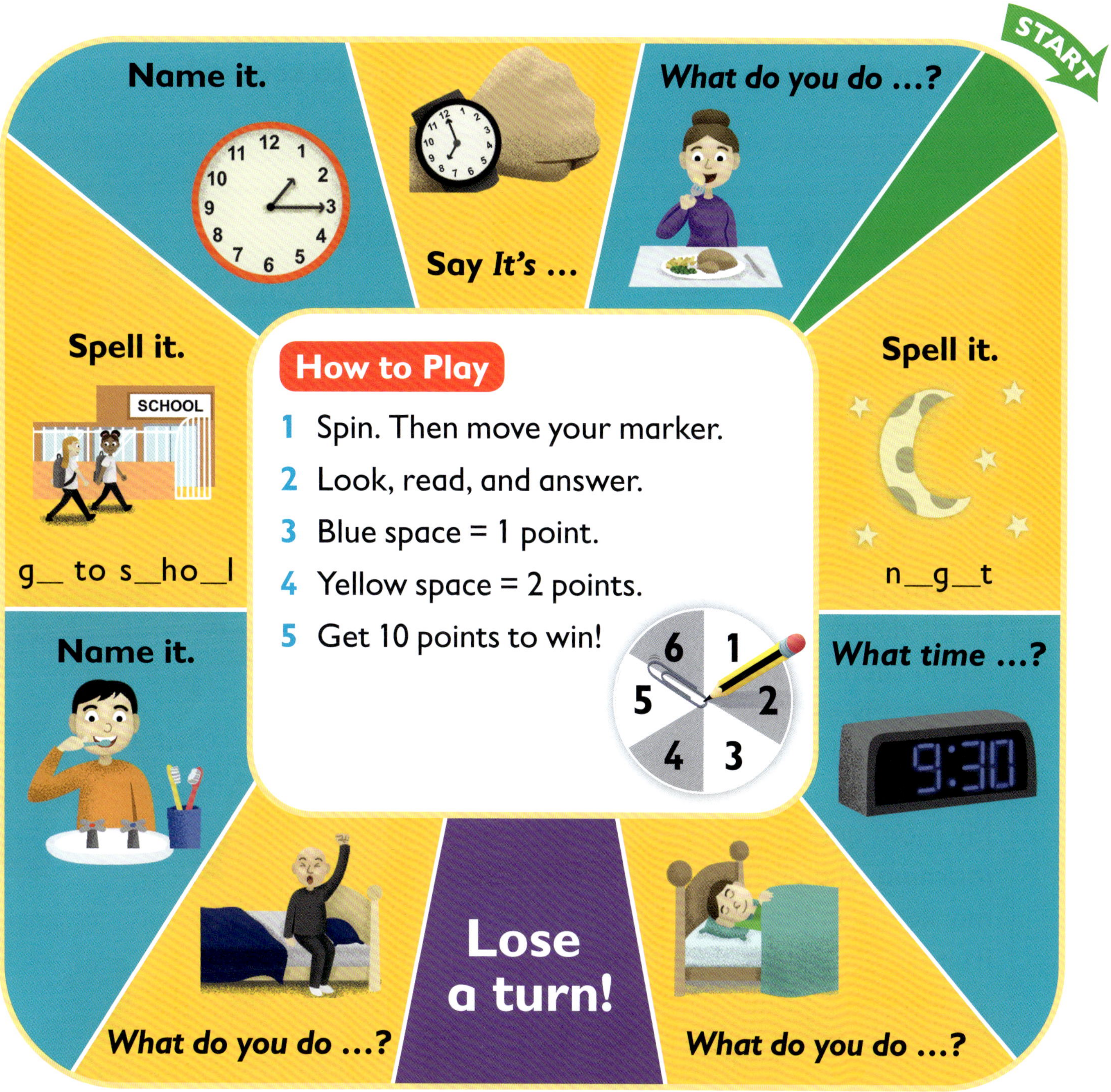

How to Play

1 Spin. Then move your marker.
2 Look, read, and answer.
3 Blue space = 1 point.
4 Yellow space = 2 points.
5 Get 10 points to win!

2 **Now complete your Progress Tracker in the Workbook.**

Workbook page 65

I can use the language in Unit 6. ☐

Share the World 3

Village Life, City Life

1 **Look at the pictures. Who lives in a village?**

2 (2.45) **Read the blog. How do the children go to school?**

Adventures of an English Teacher

Home | About Me | My Students

Village Life, City Life

January 16

Today's blog is by my students Trung and Linh. They write about their lives in Vietnam.

Trung's Life

Hi, I'm Trung. I'm 10 years old. I live in a small village. I go to school at half past five in the morning. I go home at half past eleven. My sister goes to school in the afternoon. I ride a boat to school.

My mom gets up at five o'clock in the morning. She goes to the market. The market is on the water. There's a lot of fruit at the market. I love my village!

Linh's Life

I'm Linh. I'm nine years old. I live in a big city. I get up at a quarter past seven. I eat rice and eggs for breakfast. I ride my bike to school.

My dad works in the city. He rides a motorcycle to work. My mom stays home with my brother and sister. We like to go to the mall and the zoo. I love the city!

3 Read and write the answers.

1 What time does Trung go to school? ______________

2 Where does Trung's mom go in the morning? ______________

3 What time does Linh get up? ______________

4 How does Linh's dad go to work? ______________

4 **Share Your World** **How do you go to school? What time do you go to school? Draw it in your Workbook.**

Workbook pages 66–67

YLE Starters

Exam Practice 3

Listening

1 3.01 **Listen and tick (✔) the box. There is one example.**

What does Anna do in the afternoon?

A ☐

B ☐

C ✔

1 What time does Nate get up?

A ☐

B ☐

C ☐

2 What animal can Bill see?

A ☐

B ☐

C ☐

3 What can the dog do?

A ☐

B ☐

C ☐

Reading and Writing

2 Read this. Choose a word from the box. Write the correct word next to numbers 1–5. There is one example.

My Grandpa

This is my grandpa. I go to the ...park... with Grandpa on Sunday. I ride my (**1**) .... and Grandpa walks.

Then we play games in the afternoon. I use the (**2**) .... and Grandpa reads a book. We can play in the yard, too. Grandpa has a black dog. We throw a (**3**) .... to the dog.

Grandpa drives an old (**4**) .... In the evening, we go home and eat (**5**) .... with my mom and dad.

Example

park

car

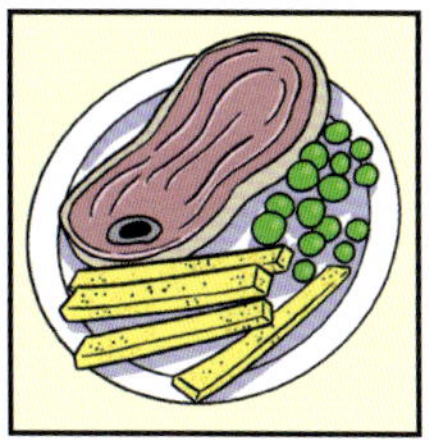

dinner

tree

computer

guitar

bike

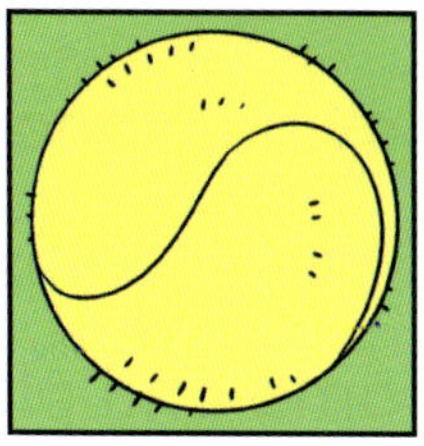

ball

7 Playtime!

Lesson 1 Vocabulary

1 **Talk about the picture.**

What's in the living room?

There's a TV.

2 3.02 **Listen, point, and say. Then quiz a friend.**

3 3.03 **Listen and point. Then chant.**

Listening to music,
Watching TV,
Reading books,
Come and read with me!

Taking photos,
Playing video games,
Playing tennis and soccer,
Come and play games!

 I can name free-time activities. ☐

Workbook page 68

Lesson 2 Grammar

1 3.04 **Listen to Dan and Nancy. Read and say.**

Grammar

What do you **like** do**ing**?
I **like** play**ing** tennis.
Do you **like** play**ing** tennis?
Yes, I **do**. **No**, I **don't**.

Grammar Practice page 109

2 3.05 **Look at the picture. Listen and say *True* or *False*.**

3 Sharebook A: page 37 B: page 37

What Do You Like Doing?

Workbook page 69

I can talk about free-time activities. ☐

Lesson 3 Story A Good Idea

1 Look and answer. Does May like listening to music?

2 3.06 **Read the story. Then act.**

Value
Play together!

3 Look, read, and write.

_______ _______ to music!

Yeah! That's a _______ _______!

I can read the story. ☐

Lesson 4 Vocabulary

1 3.07 **Listen, point, and say. Then quiz a friend.**

1 singing

2 dancing

3 writing stories

4 drawing

5 playing the piano

6 playing board games

7 baking cookies

2 3.08 **Listen and circle. Then mime and sing.**

What Do You Like Doing?

1 What do you like doing?
Do you like playing board games?
Or do you like  / 
And playing the piano?

2 What do you like doing?
Do you like baking cookies?
Or do you like  / 
And playing the piano?

3 What do you like doing?
Do you like writing stories?
Or do you like  / 
And playing the piano?

3 **Mime a favorite activity. Guess!**

Do you like playing the piano?

Yes, I do.

 I can name favorite activities. ☐ Workbook page 71

Lesson 5 Grammar

1 Listen, read, and say.

3.09

2 Listen and write check (✔) or cross (✘).

3.10

1

2

Grammar

What **does** he / she **like** do**ing**?

He / She **likes** draw**ing**.

Does he / she **like** sing**ing**?

Yes, he / she **does**.

No, he / she **doesn't**.

Grammar Practice page 109

3 Sharebook

A: page 39
B: page 41

Favorite Activities

I can ask and answer about favorite activities. ☐

Lesson 6 Music CLIL

1 **Look. How many instruments can you see?**

2 3.11 **Read the text. Which instruments have strings?**

Make Some Music!

1 Emily likes singing and playing the guitar. A guitar has six **strings**. Play the strings and make some music!

2 Kevin likes playing the piano. A piano has 52 white **keys** and 36 black keys. You can **press** the keys. The keys hit strings. The strings are inside the piano. Press the keys and make some music!

3 Steven likes playing the **flute**. There are eight **holes** in a flute. **Blow** in the flute, press your fingers on the holes, and make some music!

 I can read about musical instruments. ☐ Workbook page 73

1 Read the text again. 3.12

2 Read and circle *True* or *False*.

1 A piano has 52 white keys and 36 black keys. True / False

2 A piano doesn't have strings. True / False

3 A guitar has six strings. True / False

4 A flute has eight holes. True / False

3 Project Design a musical instrument.

4 Share it! Talk about your musical instrument.

This is my guitar. It has six strings.

Share at Home
Talk about three instruments and their sounds.

Workbook page 74

I can share my musical instrument. ☐

Lesson 8 Phonics Short vowels

1 Listen, point, and chant.
3.13

1

fan

2

nut

3

sell

4

vet

5

lock

6

fix

2 Listen and repeat. Then read and say.
3.14

1	mix	mixing	sell	yelling
2	fixing	kicking	licking	locking

REVIEW

3	dad	six	sock	wet

3 Listen, read, and say.
3.15

He is fixing the bike.

She is selling hats.

 I can read and say words with short vowel sounds. ☐ Workbook page 75

1 **Play *Spin to Win!* Use the language from Unit 7.**

How to Play

1 Spin with a pencil and paper clip.
2 Look, read, and answer.
3 Don't know? Lose a turn.
4 Get six correct answers to win!

2 **Now complete your Progress Tracker in the Workbook.**

I can use the language in Unit 7. ☐

8 Cool Clothes

Lesson 1 Vocabulary

1 Talk about the picture.

How many eyes?

Thirty-two.

2 (3.16) Listen, point, and say. Then quiz a friend.

3 (3.17) Listen and point. Then chant.

A shirt or a sweater?
Orange or blue?
Pants or a skirt?
I can't choose!

My favorite T-shirt?
Sneakers or shoes?
Red socks or white socks?
I can't choose!

 I can name clothes. ☐

Workbook page 77

Lesson 2 Grammar

1 3.18 **Listen to Nancy and Alex. Read and say.**

Grammar

Whose sweater is that?
It's **May's** sweater.
Whose sneakers are those?
They're **Dan's** sneakers.

Grammar Practice page 109

2 3.19 **Look at the picture. Listen, find, and answer.**

Whose skirt is that?

It's May's skirt.

3 **Sharebook** A: pages 43–44 B: pages 43–44

Memory Game

Whose shirt is this?

It's David's shirt. Whose sneakers are these?

Workbook page 78

I can ask and answer about clothes. ☐

Lesson 3 Story May's New Clothes

1 **Look and answer. Who helps May find her new clothes?**

2 (3.20) **Read the story. Then act.**

Value
Take care of your things.

3 Look, read, and write.

__________ put your new clothes __________!

OK!

Lesson 4 Vocabulary

1 Listen, point, and say. Then quiz a friend.

3.21

1 dress

2 jacket

3 jeans

4 shorts

5 baseball cap

6 hat

7 boots

2 Listen and circle. Then sing.

3.22

Whose Is This?

This is my dress
And my  / 
And my baseball cap.
But whose hat is this?
We know! It's Nancy's  /  !

These are my  / 
And my shorts
And my purple socks.
But whose jeans are these?
We know! They're Alex's  /  !

3 Say a clue. Then guess.

It's pink and red.

It's Lori's dress.

I can name more clothes. ☐

Workbook page 80

1 Listen, read, and say.
3.23

2 Listen and number.
3.24

Grammar

What **are** you wear**ing**?
I**'m** wear**ing** a dress.
What**'s** he / she wear**ing**?
He**'s** / She**'s** wear**ing** a hat.

Grammar Practice page 109

3 Sharebook

A: page 45
B: page 46

What's Joey Wearing?

I can ask and answer about people's clothes. ☐

Lesson 6 Art CLIL

1 **Look. What clothes can you see?**

2 (3.25) **Read the text. Who can you give old clothes to?**

Something Old, Something New

1 What can you do with **old** toys and old clothes? Here are some ideas. Don't put your old toys in the **trash**. You can give them to your brother, your sister, or a friend.

2 You can give old clothes to a store, too. But you can't give **dirty** clothes to a store. Make sure the clothes are **clean**.

3 You can use old clothes to make a toy! You can use your mom's favorite old T-shirt, your dad's old jacket, or your brother's old shorts. Look!

4 Something old can become something **new**. You can make a collage with recycled things. What **recycled** materials can you see in this collage?

I can read about recycling toys and clothes. ☐

Workbook page 82

1 Read the text again.

2 Read and write *True* or *False*.

1 You can give your toys to a young friend. ______

2 You can give dirty old clothes to a store. ______

3 You can make new things from old clothes. ______

3 Project Make a collage from recycled materials.

4 Share it! Talk about the materials in your collage.

Look! This is my sister's old dress.

Share at Home
Talk about three things you can do with old clothes.

Workbook page 83

I can share my recycled materials collage. ☐

Lesson 8 Phonics Short vowels

1 Listen, point, and chant. 3.27

1 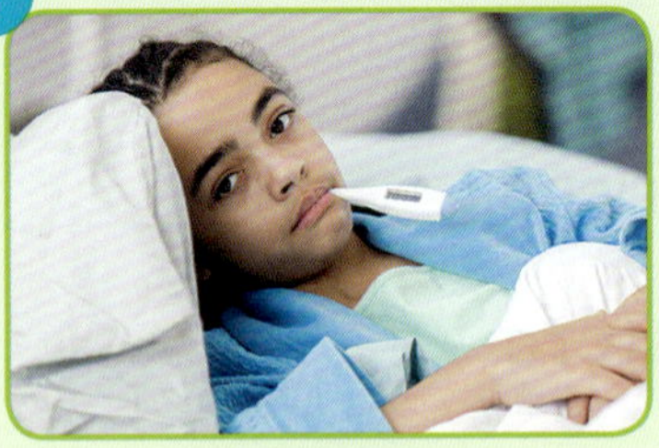
sick

2 
pan

3 
doll

4 
men

5 
hug

6 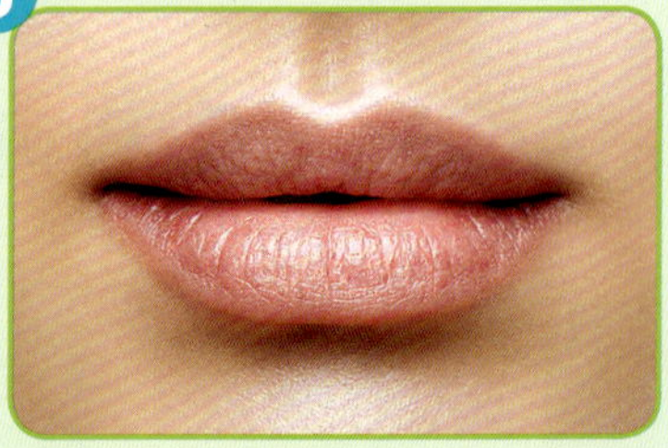
lips

2 Listen and repeat. Then read and say. 3.28

1	yell	yelled	lock	locked
2	lick	licked	mix	mixed

REVIEW

3	cat	big	box	duck

3 Listen, read, and say. 3.29

The man yells.

She locks the door.

 I can read and say words with short vowel sounds. ☐ Workbook page 84

1 Play *Race to Win!* Use the language from Unit 8.

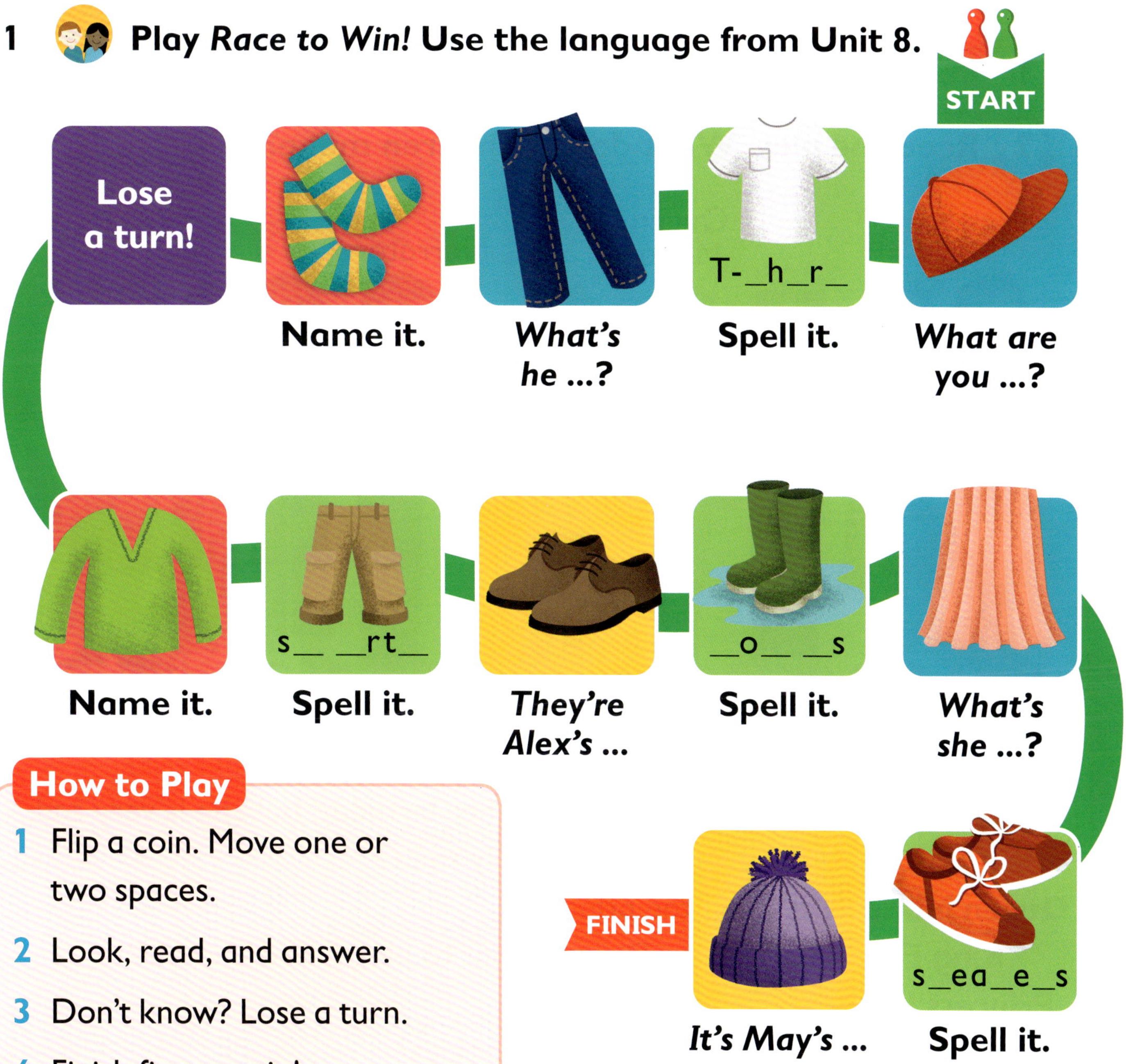

How to Play

1 Flip a coin. Move one or two spaces.

2 Look, read, and answer.

3 Don't know? Lose a turn.

4 Finish first to win!

move one space

move two spaces

2 **Now complete your Progress Tracker in the Workbook.**

Workbook page 85

I can use the language in Unit 8. ☐

Share the World 4

The Sad Princess

1 Look at the pictures. What are the characters wearing?

2 3.30 **Read the play. What do the children make?**

Narrator 1: This is Princess Lily. It's her birthday, but she is very sad.

Prince Josh: Why doesn't Princess Lily smile?

Queen Maria: Let's help the princess.

King Eric: Hi, Princess. Do you want to play a board game?

Princess Lily: No, thank you.

King Eric: Do you want to bake cookies?

Princess Lily: No, thank you.

Queen Maria: Do you like dancing, Princess Lily? I can dance. Look!

Narrator 2: The princess looks, but she doesn't smile.

Prince Josh: Do you like singing, Princess? I can sing. Listen!

Narrator 2: The princess listens, but she doesn't smile.

Narrator 1: It's Princess Lily's birthday, but she doesn't have any presents.

Narrator 2: The children want to make her a present.

Ruby: Here's an old dress!
Amy: Great!
Todd: Look! An old T-shirt!
Jack: Cool!
Ruby: Can you help?
All children: Yes! Yes, we can!
Narrator 1: The children make a new jacket from the old clothes.
Todd: Here, Princess Lily. It's a new jacket for you.
Princess Lily: Wow! Thank you!
King Eric: What are you wearing, Princess?
Princess Lily: It's my new jacket, and it's beautiful! It's from my friends. I love it!
Narrator 1: Princess Lily smiles.
Narrator 2: And everyone is happy!
All children: Happy Birthday, Princess Lily!

3 Read the play again. What do they do? Match the pictures and the sentences.

1 

2 

3 

4 

a He sings.

b She smiles.

c They make a jacket.

d She dances.

4 Share Your World **What makes you happy? Draw it in your Workbook.**

Workbook pages 86–87

Exam Practice 4

Listening

1 3.31 **Listen and color. There is one example.**

Reading and Writing

2 Look at the picture and read the questions. Write one-word answers. There are two examples.

Examples

Where are the children? on the playground

What color is the boy's T-shirt? green

Questions

1 What are the girls wearing? two ....

2 Where is the dog? next to the ....

3 What does Mom have? a ....

4 Who is pointing? the ....

5 How many children are there? ....

Grammar Practice

Unit 1 Lesson 2 (page 11)

What's	**this**? **that**?	It**'s** a horse.

Complete.

1 ________ this in my hand?
________ a spider.

2 ________ that in the tree?
________ a bird.

3 ________ ________ on the farm?
________ ________ cow.

4 ________ ________ on the chair?
________ ________ cat.

Lesson 5 (page 15)

What are	**these**? **those**?	**They're** lizard**s**.

Complete.

1 What ________ these?
________ butterflies.

2 ________ are those?
________ bees.

3 ________ ________ these?
________ mosquitos.

4 ________ ________ those?
________ frogs.

Unit 2 Lesson 2 (page 21)

That's	**his** **her**	train.
Those are	**their**	skateboard**s**.

Complete.

1 Look at the boy.
That's ________ camera.

2 Look at the girl.
That's ________ video game.

3 Look at the children.
Those are ________ scooters.

Lesson 5 (page 25)

Is this	**my** **your** **our**	bag?
Are these		pictures?

Complete.

1 Suzy, is this ________ tablet?
________, it is! Thanks!

2 Mom, is this ________ lunch?
No, it ________. It's not for you!

3 Sam, are these ________ scissors?
________, they are. We share!

Unit 3 Lesson 2 (page 35)

Is there	a tiger?	Yes, **there is**. No, **there isn't**.
Are there	hippos?	Yes, **there are**. No, **there aren't**.

Complete.

1 Is ______ a crocodile in the water?
Yes, there ______.

2 ______ there giraffes on the farm?
No, there ______.

3 Are ______ elephants at the zoo?
Yes, there ______.

4 ______ there a monkey in the tree?
No, ______ ______.

Lesson 5 (page 39)

Where's the zoo?

It's	**in front of** **behind**	the mall.
	between	the mall **and** the school.

Complete.

1 ______ the playground?
It's ______ the school.

2 ______ the beach?
It's ______ the mall and the zoo.

3 ______ the swimming pool?
It's ______ ______ ______ the zoo.

Unit 4 Lesson 2 (page 45)

Does	he she	**like** oranges?
Yes,	he	**does**.
No,	she	**doesn't**.

Complete.

1 Does Grandma ______ kiwis?
Yes, she ______.

2 ______ she like pineapples?
______, she doesn't.

3 ______ your brother like pears?
No, he ______.

4 Does he ______ bananas?
Yes, he ______.

Lesson 5 (page 49)

What **do** you **want** for dinner?

I **want** a burger and French fries, please.

Complete.

1 What ______ you want for lunch?
I ______ a sandwich, please.

2 ______ do you want for breakfast?
I ______ pancakes, ______.

3 ______ do you ______ for dinner?
______ want a burger, ______.

Unit 5 Lesson 2 (page 59)

I **can** walk **and** run.
I **can** jump, **but** I **can't** swim.

Complete.

1 I ________ draw and write.
2 The baby can walk, but he ________ run.
3 A bird ________ fly, but it ________ read.
4 A dog ________ run and swim.
5 A frog ________ fly, but it ________ jump.
6 I can ________, but I can't ________.

Lesson 5 (page 63)

Can	you he she	**sing**?	**Yes**, **No**,	I he she	**can**. **can't**.

Complete. Make true sentences.

1 ________ your dad drive a car?
________, he ________.
2 ________ you play the guitar?
________, I ________.
3 ________ your grandma use a computer?
________, she ________.

Unit 6 Lesson 2 (page 69)

What **do you do** in the	evening?
I **eat** dinner.	

Complete. Make true sentences.

1 What ________ you do in the morning?
I ________________.
2 What do you ________ in the afternoon?
I ________________.
3 What ________ in the evening?
I ________________.
4 What do you do in the ________?
I ________________.

Lesson 5 (page 73)

When **do** you **go** to bed?
I **go** to bed at 7:30.

When **does** he / she **go** to bed?
He / She **goes** to bed **at** 8:15.

Complete. Make true sentences.

1 ________ do you get up?
I ________ up at ________.
2 When ________ your mom get up?
She ________ up at ________.
3 When ________ you go to school?
I ________ to school at ________.

Unit 7 Lesson 2 (page 83)

What do you **like** do**ing**?
I **like** play**ing** soccer.

Do you **like** watch**ing** TV?
Yes, I **do**. / **No**, I **don't**.

Complete.

1 What do you like ________?
I like ________ computer games.

2 ________ you like taking photos?
Yes, I ________.

3 Do you ________ playing tennis?
No, I ________. I like ________ soccer.

Lesson 5 (page 87)

What **does** he / she **like** do**ing**?
He / She **likes** bak**ing** cookies.

Does he / she **like** draw**ing**?
Yes, he / she **does**. / **No**, he / she **doesn't**.

Complete.

1 What ________ she like doing?
She ________ dancing.

2 What does he ________ doing?
He ________ writing stories.

3 What ________ you like doing?
I like ________________.

Unit 8 Lesson 2 (page 93)

Whose sweater is that?
It's **Tom's** sweater.

Whose shoes are those?
They're **Pat's** shoes.

Complete.

1 ________ sneakers are those?
________ Lisa's sneakers.

2 Whose shirt ________ that?
________ William's shirt.

3 ________ socks are ________?
________ Sally's socks.

Lesson 5 (page 97)

What **are** you wear**ing**?
I**'m** wearing shorts.

What**'s** he / she wearing?
He**'s** / She**'s** wear**ing** a jacket.

Complete.

1 What's he ________?
________ wearing boots.

2 ________ she ________?
________ wearing a dress.

3 What ________ you ________?
________ ________ a baseball cap.

YLE words ✓ in **BOLD**

Word List

Macmillan Education Limited
4 Crinan Street
London N1 9XW

Companies and representatives throughout the world

Student Book ISBN 978-1-380-02283-7
Student Book Pack ISBN 978-1-380-02281-3

Written by Fiona Davis
Phonics lessons written by Wiley Blevins

The author has asserted their right to be identified as the author of this work in accordance with the Copyright, Designs and Patents Act 1988.

Share It! is a registered trademark published by Macmillan Education Limited

First published 2020

Designed by Pronk Media, Inc.
Illustrated by: David Belmonte (Beehive Illustration) pp. 32–33, 56–57, 80–81, 104–105; Keri Green (Beehive Illustration) pp. 18–19, 28–29, 42–43, 52–53, 66–67, 76–77, 90–91, 100–101; Patricia Lima: pp. 102–103; Emi Ordás & Wedoo Studio: pp. 4–5, 6–7, 8–9, 10–11, 12–13, 15, 20–21, 22–23, 25, 34–35, 36–37, 39, 44–45, 46–47, 49, 58–59, 60–61, 63, 68–69, 70–71, 73, 82–83, 84–85, 87, 92–93, 94-95, 97; Pablo Pino (Advocate Art) pp. 30–31; Nicholas Rudnitzky (Beehive Illustration) pp. 38–39, 48–49, 72–73, 86–87; Nicholas Rudnitzky & Gary McNamara (Beehive Illustration) pp. 14–15, 24–25, 62–63, 96–97.
Cover design by Roberto Martinez
Cover illustration by Marcin Rojek and Emi Ordás
Picture research by Sarah Wells

Author's acknowledgements
The author would like to thank the *Share It!* team for their support and encouragement.

The authors and publishers would like to thank the following for permission to reproduce their photographs: **Alamy Stock Photo**/NewStock pp. 50(t), 51(m), Alamy Stock Photo/Survivalphotos pp. 16(cl,cr); **Comstock** p. 76(bc); **Getty Images**/Getty Images/Alex Mares-Manton p. 50(br), Getty Images/Brand X Pictures/Tetra Images p. 88(t), Getty Images/Caiaimage/Martin Barraud p. 100(bl), Caiaimage/Rafal Rodzoch p. 26(bl), Getty Images/Cultura/Photo_Concepts p. 28(tc), Getty Images/DigitalVision/Jose Luis Pelaez Inc p. 23(br), Getty Images/DigitalVision/Larry Williams & Associates p. 90(bl), Getty Images/E+/Bill Oxford p. 50(background), Getty Images/E+/damircudic p. 16(br), Getty Images/E+/hadynyah pp. 42(bl), 78(tr), Getty Images/E+/kali9 p. 100(bc), Getty Images/E+/Martin Wahlborg p. 52(bl), Getty Images/E+/Pannonia p. 76(bl), Getty Images/E+/petekarici p. 26(cr), Getty Images/E+/posteriori p. 66(br), Getty Images/E+/RBFried p. 64(b), Getty Images/E+/rusm p. 66(bl), Getty Images/E+/Squaredpixels p. 28(bl), Getty Images/E+/Steve Debenport p. 100(tl), Getty Images/E+/suprun p. 66(tl), Getty Images/E+/xavierarnau p. 74(c), Getty Images/E+/yenwen p. 88(background), Getty Images/EyeEm/Andrey Mayorov p. 51(tl), Getty Images/EyeEm/Eskay Lim p. 42(tr), Getty Images/EyeEm/Nehru Sulejmanovski p. 52(tl), Getty Images/EyeEm/Philip Thompson p. 52(br), Getty Images/Fuse p. 64(background), Getty Images/Juice Images RF/Graham Oliver p. 64(c), Getty Images/Hero Images pp. 64(t), Getty Images/iStock/A_I_S p. 40(br), Getty Images/iStock/AnikaSalsera p. 98(background), Getty Images/iStock/belchonock p. 42(tc), Getty Images/iStock/Floortje p. 18(tc), Getty Images/iStock/gabes1976 p. 18(bc), Getty Images/iStock/GlobalP p. 28(tr), Getty Images/iStock/heinteh p. 100(tc), Getty Images/iStock/inarik p. 100(br), Getty Images/iStock/ivanastar p. 98(tl), Getty Images/iStock/JBryson pp. 23(bl), 52(bc), Getty Images/iStock/Laticka p. 90(tc), Getty Images/iStock/Ljupco p. 52(tr), Getty Images/iStock/LuminaStock p. 98(tr), Getty Images/iStock/Martin Leitch p. 79(cl), Getty Images/iStock/mediaphotos p. 26(background), Getty Images/iStock/Moncherie p. 50(cr), Getty Images/iStock/Samohin p. 50(cm), Getty Images/iStock/sanapadh p. 76(tl), Getty Images/iStock/shapecharge p. 66(tr), Getty Images/iStock/stockar p. 28(bc), Getty Images/iStock/stockfotocz p. 16(tr), Getty Images/iStock/stocknroll p. 42(bc), Getty Images/iStock/StockPhotosArt p. 51(tc), Getty Images/iStock/tifonimages p. 74(background), Getty Images/iStock/Toxitz p. 76(tr), Getty Images/iStock/Wavebreakmedia p. 88(b), Getty Images/iStock/wideonet p. 50(b), Getty Images/iStock/zayatssv p. 100(tr), Getty Images/iStockphoto/Thinkstock/Craig Dingle p. 18(br), Getty Images/iStockphoto/Thinkstock/Kanstantsin Shcharbinski p. 26(tr), Getty Images/J. Millar p. 52(tc), Getty Images/Jamie Grill p. 42(tl), Getty Images/Lonely Planet Images/Andrew Bain p. 79(tr), Getty Images/Mint Images RF/Mint Images - Art Wolfe p. 78(br), Getty Images/Moment Open/Anton Petrus p. 40(background), Getty Images/Moment Open/Robert Muckley p. 40(bl), Getty Images/Moment/Akiko Aoki p. 74(tl), Getty Images/Moment/Alan Vernon p. 40(tr), Getty Images/Moment/mikroman6 pp. 16(background), 66(tc), Getty Images/Moment/Oscar Sánchez Photography p. 16(bl), Getty Images/Moment/Paulo Amorim p. 28(br), Getty Images/Moment/Pierre Ogeron p. 74(cb), Getty Images/Moment/Tomekbudujedomek p. 28(tl), Getty Images/Photodisc/Mark Deeble and Victoria Stone p. 40(tr, inset), Getty Images/Photodisc/Roy JAMES Shakespeare p. 88(c), Getty Images/Photographers Choice/Andrew Holt p. 78(cl), Getty Images/RubberBall Productions p. 18(tr), Getty Images/Sam Diephuis p. 18(bl), Getty Images/SCIENCE PHOTO LIBRARY/KTSDESIGN p. 90(tl), Getty Images/Tetra Images p. 90(bc), Getty Images/Tom Chance p. 18(tl), Getty Images/Westend61 p. 66(bc); **ImageSource** p. 74b; **Photodisc**/Thinkstock Images p. 76(br); **Shutterstock**/cunaplus p. 90(tr), Shutterstock/Elena Rostunova p. 51(tr), Shutterstock/smspsy p. 50(cr), Shutterstock/spass p. 74(tr), Shutterstock/Tatevosian Yana p. 76(tc), Shutterstock/travelview p. 42(br), Shutterstock/Vitaly Korovin p. 16(magnifying glass), Shutterstock/wk1003mike p. 90(br); **Macmillan Education Limited** p. 98(br)

Commissioned photographs by Kikor (pp. 11, 15, 21, 25, 35, 39, 45, 49, 59, 63, 69, 73, 83, 87, 93, 97).

The authors and publishers wish to thank the following for their help with the photo shoot: World of Kids, Inc.; Athena; Ben; Bianca; Jayden; Logan; and Maggie.

Commissioned prop photographs by Luise Johnson-Dailey, Bluwave Creative (pp. 17, 27, 41, 51, 65, 75, 89, 99).

Printed and bound in Brazil.
2025
65